ANIMALS

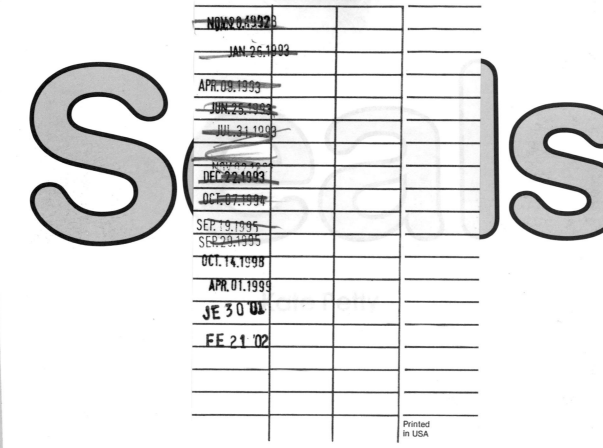

Seals

BARRON'S

The rookery

Seals are mammals that live in the sea. But when it is time to have their babies they come ashore in great numbers. A beach full of seals is called a rookery. There are two main groups of seals. "Eared" seals have ear flaps you can see and strong front flippers. "True" seals don't have ear flaps and their front flippers are not much use on land.

Bulls arrive at the rookery first to claim a space for themselves and any females they can attract.

A crowded rookery of Northern Fur seals ▷

Newborn

The mother seal finds a dip or hollow in which to have her single pup. As soon as it is born the mother sniffs and cleans the pup all over so that she becomes familiar with its particular smell. The newborn pup has a woolly coat of fur and its large eyes are wide open. It can move about a little bit, but it depends entirely on its mother for food in the form of her rich milk.

Newborn Ringed seal pup with its mother

This Weddell seal gets to know her newborn pup's special smell. ▷

Early days

Seal pups are either asleep or hungry. When a mother goes into the sea to catch fish for herself the pup bleats pitifully until she returns to feed it. Even when the beach is crowded with pups, the mother recognizes her own baby by its cry and its smell. This is important because if a pup became separated from its mother it would soon starve to death.

A hungry pup calls for its mother.

A mother Elephant seal suckling her pup ▷

Life without a mother

Some sea mammals spend several months bringing up their young. Most "true" seal mothers, such as Gray seals, feed their babies for about three weeks. When the babies have built up a good store of fat to live on the mothers leave them to manage on their own. At this age the pups are just losing their baby fur. They haven't tried to swim or to feed themselves yet.

The pup's coat is beginning to change.

A three-week-old Gray seal pup has tripled *its* **birth weight.** ▷

Learning and playing

The abandoned seal pups have to learn very quickly otherwise they will not survive. They test the water in rock pools before going into the open sea. The pups are wary of the water at first, but soon they enjoy splashing about in the pools together. Once the seal pups can swim, they attempt to catch fish for themselves. Sheer hunger makes them learn quickly.

Swimming is fun once you know how.

Soon this pup will play happily in the open sea. ▷

Feeding

Seals are carnivores. Most seals eat fish and other sea creatures such as squid and shellfish. Fierce Leopard seals have sharp teeth and prey on penguins and other baby seals. Crab-eater seals also have sharp pointed teeth, but these are for straining tiny shrimps, called krill. A seal grips a fish with its front flippers and usually eats it all except for the head.

Crab-eater seals don't actually eat crabs!

A seal with its catch ▷

Life at sea

The seal pups soon become experts at swimming and diving. The hind flippers which make "true" seals so clumsy on land propel them along with powerful side-to-side movements. They use their front flippers mostly for steering. "Eared" seals use their front flippers to move about in the water rather as they do on land. You probably find it hard work to hold your breath underwater for one minute, but most seals can stay underwater for 10 or even 20 minutes.

Flippers are better for swimming than walking.

An "eared" seal swimming ▷

Bedtime

Seals can even sleep in the water. They sleep floating vertically – rather like a bottle bobbing up and down in the water. At other times they lie just below the surface, rising only to breathe, sleeping all the time. Some seals also like to haul themselves out on the rocks and sleep in the sun. "Eared" seals like this fur seal spend more time on land than "true" seals.

Seals "bottling"

A cold wave has woken this Fur seal from its nap in the sun. ▷

Seal senses

The seal's good sense of smell is not much use underwater. They use their strong whiskers to help them "feel" when fish are nearby. Hearing is their most important sense. In a way similar to bats, many seals use "echo location" to find prey by making high pitched noises that bounce off nearby objects. With their large eyes seals can see well underwater. Their pupils dilate to let in as much light as possible.

A seal uses its good sense of hearing to recognize another's call.

The seal's strong whiskers are called "vibrissae." ▷

Seals around the world

All true seals live in cold water except for the Monk seal. Harp seals, Ringed seals, Hooded seals, Ribbon seals and Bearded seals all live in the icy Arctic. The Gray seal and the Common seal live in the slightly warmer waters of the North Atlantic and the North Pacific. Elephant seals from the Pacific coast of North America and islands in the South Atlantic are twice as big as other seals.

These seals live in the Antarctic apart from the Harp seal which is found in the Arctic.

Leopard seal

Weddell seal

Ross seal

Crab-eater seal

Harp seal

Monk seals live in the warm waters of the Mediterranean and around tropical islands. ▷

Seal facts

A newborn Gray seal weighs about 30 lb and measures 30 in from the top of its head to the tip of its hind flippers. After one week it weighs twice as much and at three weeks its weight is 110 lb. Adult male seals weigh about 600 lb. They reach maturity at about six years old. Adult females weigh 300 lb. They are mature at four years old but are not ready to have their own pups until a year or so later.

Newborn

Adult female

Adult male

Index

Photographic Credits:

Cover and pages 3, 7,15 and 21: Bruce Coleman Photo Library; pages 5, 17 and 19: Planet Earth Pictures; pages 9 and 11: Frank Lane Picture Agency; page 13: Zefa.

Design	David West Children's Book Design
Illustrations	George Thompson
Picture Research	Emma Krikler

The publishers wish to thank Claire Robinson, Education Officer at London Zoo, for her assistance in the preparation of this book.

First paperback edition for the United States and Canada published 1992 by Barron's Educational Series, Inc.

First published in the United States 1991 by Gloucester Press.
© Copyright 1990 by Aladdin Books Ltd

All inquiries should be addressed to:
Barron's Educational Series, Inc.
250 Wireless Boulevard
Hauppauge, New York 11788

Library of Congress
Catalog Card No. 90-44926
International Standard
Book No. 0-8120-4970-5

Library of Congress Cataloging-in-Publication Data

Petty, Kate.
    Seals / Kate Petty.
    p. cm.--(Baby animals)
    Includes index.
    Summary: Portrays the lives of seal pups around the world, describing their birth, diet, behavior, and life at sea.
  ISBN 0-8120-4970-5 (paperback)
1. Seals (Animals)--Infancy--Juvenile literature. (1. Seals (Animals) 2. animals--Infancy.) I. Title. II. Series: Petty, Kate. Baby animals.
QL737.P64P47 1991
599.74'5--dc20   90-44926 CIP AC

Printed in Belgium
2345   987654321